Writing Prompts Using Pictures:

Text Types for Kids

Point of View

Narrative

How to

Information Animals

Use colorful photographs to practice writing.
By: Ellie Tiemann

© A World of Language Learners 2024. All rights reserved.
All rights reserved. No part of this publication may be reproduced, distributed, or transmitted in any form or by any means. This includes photocopying, recording, or other electronic or mechanical methods without prior permission of the publisher, except in the case of brief quotations embodied in critical reviews and other noncommercial uses permitted by copyright law.

No part of this product maybe used or reproduced for commercial use.

Contact the author :
aworldoflanguagelearners@gmail.com

Table of Contents	Page
Teacher Guides	5
Narrative Writing Prompts	7
How to	25
Information Animals	57
Point of View	83

 Narrative Writing Prompts

Narrative Writing Prompts

Narrative writing tells a story.

Include a beginning, middle, and ending.

Use transition words: first, next, then, after that, finally, last.

Add in details to make the story interesting.

📖 Narrative Writing Prompts

Word Bank

beach	dig
sand	sunny
bucket	wet
shovel	fun
water	fill
wash away	

Transition Words

First	Next
Then	After that
Finally	Last

Write a story about a kid building a sandcastle.

The kid went to the _____.
He/she/they played with _____.
It was _____.
He/she/they had _____.

_____
_____
_____
_____
_____
_____
_____

© A World of Language Learners

Narrative Writing Prompts

Word Bank

water	jump
fountain	spray
splash	wet
towel	dry
play	exciting
fun	

Transition Words

First	Next
Then	After that
Finally	Last

Write a story about kids playing in a water fountain.

The kids went to the _____.
They played with _____.
It was _____.
They had _____.

_____
_____
_____
_____
_____
_____
_____

© A World of Language Learners

Narrative Writing Prompts

Word Bank

alien	fight
people	help
earth	new
talk	fun
woods	beach

Transition Words

First	Next
Then	After that
Finally	
	Last

Write a story about what happens when an alien comes to earth.

An alien came to _____.

It went to _____.

It was _____.

It had _____.

_____
_____
_____
_____
_____
_____
_____
_____

Narrative Writing Prompts

Word Bank

treasure	boxes
money	carry
open	rich
hunt	heavy
excited	shiny

Transition Words

First	Next
Then	After that
Finally	Last

Write a story about finding a treasure box.

I found a _____.
It looked _____.
It was _____.
It had _____.

_____
_____
_____
_____
_____
_____
_____
_____

© A World of Language Learners

Narrative Writing Prompts

Word Bank

pool	dog
swimming	splash
goggles	water
towel	slide
outside	wet

Write a story about a day at the pool.

Transition Words

First	Next
Then	After that
Finally	Last

I went to the _____.
I went _____.
I got _____.
I had _____.

_____
_____
_____
_____
_____
_____
_____
_____

Narrative Writing Prompts

Word Bank

ice skating	fast
skating rink	fall
exciting	fun
lace	cold
help	tie
slow	cone

Transition Words

First	Next
Then	After that
Finally	Last

Write a story about learning how to ice skate.

I went to the _____.
I went _____.
It was _____.
I had _____

Narrative Writing Prompts

Write a story about two dogs going to a party.

Word Bank	
dogs	hat
party	fun
dance	friends
tie	music
food	meat

Transition Words	
First	Next
Then	After that
Finally	
	Last

The _____ went to a _____ .
They saw _____.
They smelled _____.
They had _____.

_____
_____
_____
_____
_____
_____
_____
_____

Narrative Writing Prompts

Word Bank

beach	swim
bucket	dig
sandcastle	wet
towel	cold
crab	build

Transition Words

First	Next
Then	After that
Finally	Last

Write a story about going to the beach.

I went _____.

I saw _____.

I made _____.

I had _____.

_____
_____
_____
_____
_____
_____
_____

© A World of Language Learners

Narrative Writing Prompts

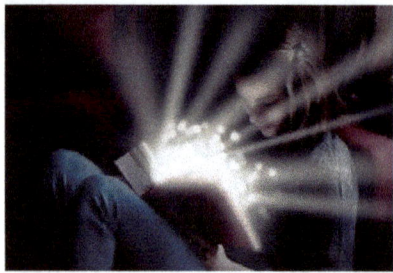

Word Bank

boat	sky
fly	new
wings	land
little	story
big	water
travel	fast

Transition Words

First	Next
Then	After that
Finally	Last

Write a story about a magical boat.

Look at the _____.
It can _____.
It looks _____.
It went _____.

_____
_____
_____
_____
_____
_____
_____

Narrative Writing Prompts

Write a story about a castle in the clouds.

Word Bank	
clouds	sky
alone	fly
high	castle
cold	big
rooms	white

Transition Words	
First	Next
Then	After that
Finally	Last

Look at the _____.
It looks _____.
It has _____.
It can _____.

_____
_____
_____
_____
_____
_____
_____
_____

📖 Narrative Writing Prompts

Word Bank

animals	goat
gorilla	lion
interesting	feeding
panda	looking
quacking	walking
exciting	ducks

Transition Words

First	Next
Then	After that
Finally	Last

Write a story about a day at the zoo.

I went to the _____.

I saw _____.

I heard _____.

It was _____.

_____
_____
_____
_____
_____
_____
_____

Narrative Writing Prompts

Word Bank

baseball	run
bat	catch
throw	play
hit	fun
cheers	exciting

Write a story about playing a baseball game.

Transition Words

First	Next
Then	After that
Finally	Last

I like to play _____.
I can _____.
I hear _____.
It is _____.

_____
_____
_____
_____
_____
_____
_____
_____

📖 Narrative Writing Prompts

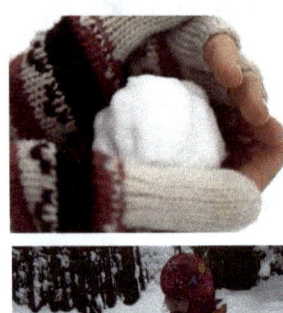

Word Bank

snowball	stick
scarf	roll
carrot	stack
cold	tall
snowman	big
snowwoman	kids

Transition Words

First	Next
Then	After that
Finally	Last

Write a story about a day making a snowman.

I like to make a _____.
First get _____.
Then add _____.
It looks _____.

_____
_____
_____
_____
_____
_____
_____
_____

Narrative Writing Prompts

Word Bank

roller coaster	fun
Ferris wheel	train
bumper cars	riding
around	tickets
playing	swings

Transition Words

First	Next
Then	After that
Finally	Last

Write a story about going to an amusement park.

The kids went to an_____.
They went to_____.
They heard_____.
It was _____.

_____
_____
_____
_____
_____
_____
_____

Narrative Writing Prompts

Write a story about going camping.

Word Bank
sleeping bag	guitar
lantern	roast
campfire	tent
stove	sleep
cook	hike

Transition Words
First	Next
Then	After that
Finally	Last

The kids went_____.
They made a _____.
They heard_____.
It was _____.

_____
_____
_____
_____
_____
_____
_____
_____

Narrative Writing Prompts

Word Bank

books	jump
wet	careful
puddle	mud
splash	water
jacket	slippery

Transition Words

First	Next
Then	After that
Finally	Last

Write a story about playing in the rain.

When it rains I can _____.
I see _____.
I hear _____.
I feel _____.

_____
_____
_____
_____
_____
_____
_____
_____

How to Writing Prompts

How to writing tells the reader how to make or do something.

Write the steps in order.

Use transition words: first, next, then, after that, finally, last.

Include details so that the reader knows what to do for each step.

How to Writing Prompts

Word Bank

basketball	foul
net	practice
court	foul
hoop	dribble
referee	shoot
shoes	pass

Transition Words

First	Next
Then	After that
Finally	Last

Write about how to play basketball. Describe the equipment you need to play.

The equipment that you need to play basketball is/are _____.
This is how to play basketball _____.

_____
_____
_____
_____
_____
_____
_____
_____

How to Writing Prompts

Word Bank

baseball	umpire
bat	hit
plate	pitcher
practice	mitt
foul	coach

Transition Words

First	Next
Then	After that
Finally	Last

Write how to play baseball. Describe the equipment you need to play.

The equipment that you need to play baseball is/are _____.
This is how to play baseball _____.

_____
_____
_____
_____
_____
_____
_____
_____

How to Writing Prompts

Word Bank

kick board	kick
goggles	float
floaties	jump
swim	dive
splash	noodle

Transition Words

First	Next
Then	After that
Finally	Last

Write how to play in a pool. Describe the equipment you need to play.

The equipment that you need to play in a pool is/are _____.
This is how to play in a pool _____.

_____
_____
_____
_____
_____
_____
_____
_____

How to Writing Prompts

Word Bank

leash	water
bowl	walk
food	play
bone	brush
ball	run
toy	drink

Transition Words

First	Next
Then	After that
Finally	
	Last

Write how to take care of a pet dog. Describe the equipment you need.

The equipment that you need to take care of a pet dog is/are _____. This is how to take care of a pet dog _____.

_____
_____
_____
_____
_____
_____
_____

How to Writing Prompts

Word Bank

climb	lick
drink	litter box
bowl	collar
water	pet
food	eat

Transition Words

First	Next
Then	After that
Finally	Last

Write how to take care of a pet cat. Describe the equipment you need.

The equipment that you need to take care of a pet cat is/are _____. This is how to take care of a pet cat _____.

_____
_____
_____
_____
_____
_____
_____

© A World of Language Learners

How to Writing Prompts

Word Bank

water	bowl
swim	tank
clean	plants
food	net

Transition Words

First	Next
Then	After that
Finally	
	Last

Write how to take care of a pet fish. Describe the equipment you need.

The equipment that you need to take care of a pet fish is/are _____. This is how to take care of a pet fish _____.

_____
_____
_____
_____
_____
_____
_____

How to Writing Prompts

Word Bank

food	fly
cadge	clean
water	branch
bowl	toy
straw	feathers

Write how to take care of a pet bird. Describe the equipment you need.

Transition Words

First　Next
Then　After that
Finally
　　　Last

The equipment that you need to take care of a pet bird is/are _____. This is how to take care of a pet bird _____.

_____
_____
_____
_____
_____
_____
_____

How to Writing Prompts

Word Bank

bun	onion
burger	cut
cook	knife
tomato	stack
lettuce	heat
grill	eat

Transition Words

First	Next
Then	After that
Finally	Last

Write how to make a burger. Describe the ingredients and equipment you need.

The equipment that you need to make a burger is/are _____. The ingredients that you need is/are _____. This is how to make a burger _____.

_____
_____
_____
_____
_____
_____
_____
_____

How to Writing Prompts

Word Bank

milk	open
spoon	box
cereal	eat
bowl	fruit
pour	cut
mix	knife

Transition Words

First	Next
Then	After that
Finally	Last

Write how to make a bowl of cereal. Describe the ingredients and equipment you need.

The equipment that you need to make a bowl of cereal is/are _____. The ingredients that you need is/are _____. This is how to make a bowl of cereal _____.

_____
_____
_____
_____
_____
_____
_____
_____

How to Writing Prompts

Word Bank

banana	apple
orange	cut
grapes	peel
strawberries	bowl
blueberries	spoon
cutting board	knife

Transition Words

First	Next
Then	After that
Finally	Last

Write how to make a fruit salad. Describe the ingredients and equipment you need.

The equipment that you need to make a fruit salad is/are _____. The ingredients that you need is/are _____. This is how to make a fruit salad _____.

_____
_____
_____
_____
_____
_____
_____

How to Writing Prompts

Word Bank

mix	oil
stir	pour
bake	hot
flour	milk
eggs	bowl
berries	oven

Transition Words

First   Next
Then   After that
Finally
        Last

Write how to make muffins. Describe the ingredients and equipment you need.

The equipment that you need to make muffins is/are _____. The ingredients that you need is/are _____. This is how to make muffins _____.

_____
_____
_____
_____
_____
_____
_____
_____

How to Writing Prompts

Word Bank

helmet	balance
air pump	turn
bike	peddle
ride	fast
tire	slow

Transition Words

First	Next
Then	After that
Finally	Last

Write how to ride a bike. Describe the equipment you need.

The equipment that you need to ride a bike is/are _____. This is how to ride a bike _____.

_____
_____
_____
_____
_____
_____
_____

© A World of Language Learners

How to Writing Prompts

Word Bank

helmet	turn
scooter	steer
ramp	bump
ride	fast
push	handlebar
wheels	trick

Transition Words

First	Next
Then	After that
Finally	Last

Write how to ride a scooter. Describe the equipment you need.

The equipment that you need to ride a scooter is/are _____. This is how to ride a scooter _____.

_____
_____
_____
_____
_____
_____
_____

© A World of Language Learners

How to Writing Prompts

Word Bank

skateboard	jump
helmet	fast
ramp	high
jump	trick
balance	push

Transition Words

First	Next
Then	After that
Finally	Last

Write how to ride a skateboard. Describe the equipment you need.

The equipment that you need to ride a skateboard is/are _____. This is how to ride a skateboard _____.

_____
_____
_____
_____
_____
_____
_____
_____

© A World of Language Learners

How to Writing Prompts

Word Bank

blocks	connect
Legos	high
small	fall
stack	rectangle
balance	cube
long	prism

Transition Words

First	Next
Then	After that
Finally	
	Last

Write how to build a block tower. Describe the equipment you need.

The equipment that you need to build a block tower is/are _____.
This is how to build a block tower.

_____
_____
_____
_____
_____
_____
_____

© A World of Language Learners

How to Writing Prompts

Word Bank

pieces	tunnel
connect	straight
wooden	curved
plastic	high
train	circle

Transition Words

First	Next
Then	After that
Finally	Last

Write how to build a toy train track. Describe the equipment you need.

The equipment that you need to build a toy train track is/are _____. This is how to build a toy train track _____.

_____
_____
_____
_____
_____
_____
_____
_____

How to Writing Prompts

Word Bank	
sand	dump
shovel	wave
bucket	pack
water	stack
shells	wet
fill	high

Transition Words	
First	Next
Then	After that
Finally	Last

Write how to build a sandcastle. Describe the equipment you need.

The equipment that you need to build a sandcastle is/are _____. This is how to build a sandcastle _____.

_____
_____
_____
_____
_____
_____
_____
_____

How to Writing Prompts

Word Bank

snowball	scarf
roll	pack
stack	small
carrot	large
stick	hat
cold	gloves

Transition Words

First	Next
Then	After that
Finally	Last

Write how to build a snowman. Describe the equipment you need.

The equipment that you need to build a snowman is/are _____. This is how to build a snowman _____.

_____
_____
_____
_____
_____
_____
_____
_____

How to Writing Prompts

Word Bank	
shuffle	take
pass	higher
match	ace
go	queen
fish	king
numbers	jack

Transition Words	
First	Next
Then	After that
Finally	Last

Write how to play cards. What are the rules and how do you win the game?

The rules to play the _____. card game are _____. This is how to play the _____ card game _____.

_____
_____
_____
_____
_____
_____
_____
_____

How to Writing Prompts

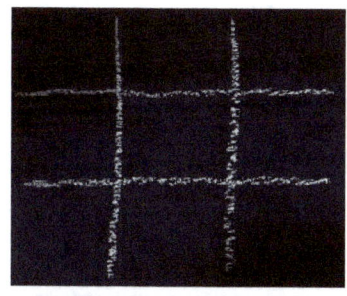

Word Bank	
board	over
lines	three
X	row
O	connect
jump	write

Transition Words	
First	Next
Then	After that
Finally	Last

Write how to play tic-tac-toe. What are the rules and how do you win the game?

The rules to play tic-tac-toe are _____.
This is how to play tic-tac-toe _____.

_____
_____
_____
_____
_____
_____
_____

How to Writing Prompts

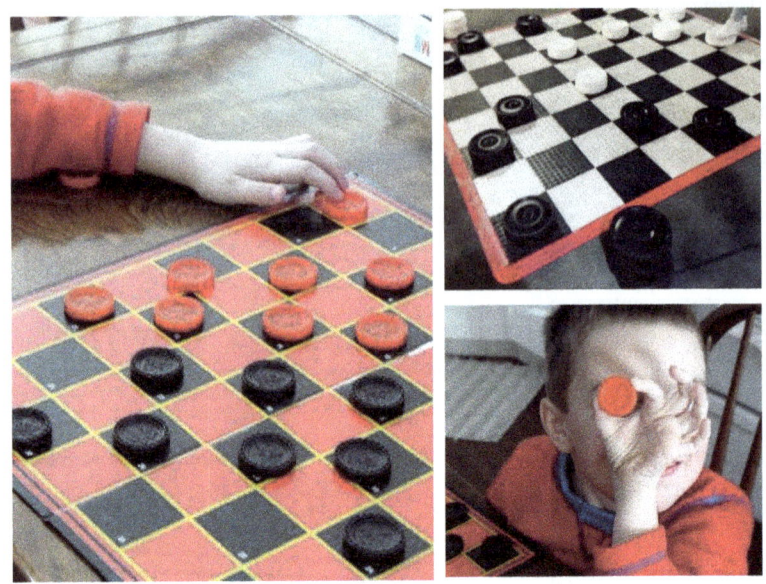

Word Bank

piece	jump
checker	opponent
red	capture
black	diagonally
player	across

Transition Words

First	Next
Then	After that
Finally	Last

Write how to play checkers. What are the rules and how do you win the game?

The rules to play checkers are _____.
This is how to play checkers _____.

_____
_____
_____
_____
_____
_____
_____

How to Writing Prompts

Word Bank

piece	draw
dice	capture
move	turn
jump	player
roll	skip
card	back
board	forward

Transition Words

First	Next
Then	After that
Finally	
	Last

Write how to play a board game. What are the rules and how do you win the game?

The rules to play the _____. board game are _____. This is how to play the _____ board game _____.

_____
_____
_____
_____
_____
_____
_____
_____

How to Writing Prompts

Word Bank

plate	bowl
cup	right
knife	left
fork	top
spoon	food
napkin	place

Transition Words

First	Next
Then	After that
Finally	Last

Write how to set the table. Describe the items you need.

The items that you need to set the table are _____. This is how to set the table _____.

_____
_____
_____
_____
_____
_____
_____
_____

How to Writing Prompts

Word Bank

hat	mittens
coat	pants
boots	warm
scarf	wrap
gloves	zip

Transition Words

First	Next
Then	After that
Finally	Last

Write how to dress to go out in the snow. Describe the items you need.

The items that you need to go out in the snow are _____. This is how to dress to go out in the snow _____.

_____
_____
_____
_____
_____
_____
_____

© A World of Language Learners

How to Writing Prompts

Word Bank	
umbrella	zip
boots	open
jacket	wet
hat	rubber
pants	waterproof

Write how to dress to go out in the rain. Tell about the items you need.

Transition Words	
First	Next
Then	After that
Finally	
	Last

The items that you need to go out in the rain are _____. This is how to dress to go out in the rain _____.

_____
_____
_____
_____
_____
_____
_____

How to Writing Prompts

Word Bank

balloons	plates
streamers	forks
hats	piñata
banner	colorful
cups	drawings

Transition Words

First	Next
Then	After that
Finally	
	Last

Write how to decorate for a party. Describe the items you need.

The items that you need to decorate for a party are _____. This is how to decorate for a party _____.

_____
_____
_____
_____
_____
_____
_____

How to Writing Prompts

Word Bank

dough	spoon
sauce	pan
bake	oven
cheese	rolling
spread	pin
cut	topping

Transition Words

First	Next
Then	After that
Finally	Last

Write how to make a pizza. Describe the ingredients and equipment you need.

The equipment that you need to make a pizza is/are _____. The ingredients that you need is/are _____. This is how to make a pizza _____.

_____
_____
_____
_____
_____
_____
_____

How to Writing Prompts

Word Bank

blender	juice
cup	cut
straw	knife
fruit	banana
milk	pineapple
pour	berries

Transition Words

First	Next
Then	After that
Finally	Last

Write how to make a smoothie. Describe the ingredients and equipment you need.

The equipment that you need to make a smoothie is/are _____. The ingredients that you need is/are _____. This is how to make a smoothie _____.

_____
_____
_____
_____
_____
_____
_____
_____

© A World of Language Learners

How to Writing Prompts

Word Bank

kernels	butter
air	bag
popper	bowl
pot	microwave
cook	open
hot	pop
oil	salt

Write how to make popcorn. Describe the ingredients and equipment you need.

Transition Words

First   Next

Then   After that

Finally

Last

The equipment that you need to make popcorn is/are _____. The ingredients that you need is/are _____. This is how to make popcorn _____.

_____
_____
_____
_____
_____
_____
_____
_____

How to Writing Prompts

Word Bank

flour	bowl
eggs	bake
banana	oven
chocolate	pan
spoon	plate
mix	whisk

Write how to make cookies. Describe the ingredients and equipment you need.

Transition Words

First	Next
Then	After that
Finally	Last

The equipment that you need to make cookies is/are _____. The ingredients that you need is/are _____. This is how to make cookies _____.

_____
_____
_____
_____
_____
_____
_____
_____

Information Animal Writing Prompts

Information writing tells facts.

Include a main idea.

Add in supporting details.

Information Animal Writing Prompts

Word Bank

nut	white
tree	ears
tail	claws
fur	paws
brown	branch
	woods

Write information about the squirrel.

The squirrel eats _____. It lives _____. This is how it looks; it has _____.

© A World of Language Learners

Information Animal Writing Prompts

Word Bank

nectar	black
antenna	white
tongue	warm
wing	blosso
orange	ming
	flower

Write information about the butterfly.

It lives _____. This is how it looks; it has _____.

_____
_____
_____
_____
_____
_____
_____

Information Animal Writing Prompts

Word Bank

tree	fur
woods	brown
forest	large
leaves	nose
plants	eyes
antlers	ears

Write information about the moose.

The moose eats _____. It lives _____. This is how it looks; it has _____.

_____
_____
_____
_____
_____
_____
_____
_____

Information Animal Writing Prompts

Word Bank

fur	leaves
black	nose
fluffy	hands
grass	legs
plant	eyes
tree	head
jungle	fingers

Write information about the gorilla.

The gorilla eats _____. It lives _____. This is how it looks; it has _____.

_____
_____
_____
_____
_____
_____
_____
_____

Information Animal Writing Prompts

Word Bank

foal	stripes
milk	white
nursing	black
grass	legs
grassland	head
small	mouth

Write information about the baby zebra.

The baby zebra drinks _____. It lives _____. This is how it looks; it has _____.

_____
_____
_____
_____
_____
_____
_____
_____

© A World of Language Learners

Information Animal Writing Prompts

Word Bank

leaves	black
plant	white
wood	ears
tree	paws
woods	eyes
fur	nose

Write information about the panda.

The panda eats _____. It lives _____. This is how it looks; it has _____.

_____
_____
_____
_____
_____
_____
_____
_____

© A World of Language Learners

Information Animal Writing Prompts

Word Bank

stripes	legs
black	hoofs
white	grass
ears	grassland
mouth	dry
grass	large

Write information about the zebra.

The zebra eats _____. It lives _____. This is how it looks; it has _____.

_____
_____
_____
_____
_____
_____
_____

Information Animal Writing Prompts

Word Bank

meat	brown
tree	white
beak	yellow
feathers	eye
feather	claws

Write information about the eagle.

The eagle eats _____. It lives _____. This is how it looks; it has _____.

_____
_____
_____
_____
_____
_____
_____

Information Animal Writing Prompts

Word Bank

meat	tree
gazelle	grassland
spots	large
orange	paws
black	mouth
white	eye
branch	ears

Write information about the leopard.

The leopard eats _____. It lives _____. This is how it looks; it has _____.

_____

_____

_____

_____

_____

_____

_____

_____

Information Animal Writing Prompts

Word Bank

tongue	ears
leaves	mouth
savanna	eye
spots	long
brown	neck
white	large
woodlands	tree

Write information about the giraffe.

The giraffe eats _____. It lives _____. This is how it looks; it has _____.

_____
_____
_____
_____
_____
_____
_____

Information Animal Writing Prompts

Word Bank

worm	eyes
mother	orange
bird	gray
feed	pink
beak	nest

Write information about the chicks.

The chicks eat _____. It lives _____. This is how it looks; it has _____.

_____
_____
_____
_____
_____
_____
_____

Information Animal Writing Prompts

Word Bank

grass	eye
fur	ears
brown	legs
mouth	tail
nose	woods

Write information about the kangaroo.

The kangaroo eats _____. It lives _____. This is how it looks; it has _____.

_____
_____
_____
_____
_____
_____
_____

Information Animal Writing Prompts

Word Bank

shell	lay
tentacle	leaf
brow	green
head	eggs
mouth	black

Write information about the snail.

The snail is _____. This is how it looks; it has _____.

_____
_____
_____
_____
_____
_____
_____

Information Animal Writing Prompts

Word Bank

shedding	blue
skin	green
molt	legs
old	wings
new	head
brown	thorax
abdomen	grass

Write information about the dragonfly.

The dragonfly is _____. This is how it looks; it has _____.

_____
_____
_____
_____
_____
_____
_____
_____

Information Animal Writing Prompts

Word Bank

hatching	head
crack	eyes
eggshell	scales
white	feet
brown	hard
shell	soft

Write information about the tortoise.

The desert tortoise is _____. This is how it looks; it has _____.

_____
_____
_____
_____
_____
_____
_____
_____

Information Animal Writing Prompts

Word Bank

eggs	yellow
hatch	white
open	feet
shell	eyes
orange	walk
black	dots

Write information about the leaf bugs.

The leaf bugs are _____. This is how they look; they have _____.

_____
_____
_____
_____
_____
_____
_____

Information Animal Writing Prompts

Word Bank

following	brown
short	water
feathers	long
swimming	parents
black	soft
white	lake

Write information about the geese.

The geese are _____. They live _____. This is how they look; they have _____.

_____
_____
_____
_____
_____
_____
_____

Information Animal Writing Prompts

Word Bank

flying	white
jumping	black
orange	beak
feathers	wings

Write information about the puffins.

The puffins are _____. This is how they look; they have _____.

_____
_____
_____
_____
_____
_____
_____
_____

Information Animal Writing Prompts

Word Bank

galloping	brown
majestic	black
running	head
fast	ear
water	legs
strong	tail
hoofs	wet

Write information about the horses.

The horses are _____. This is how they look; they have _____.

_____
_____
_____
_____
_____
_____
_____

Information Animal Writing Prompts

Word Bank

walking	trunks
water	long
tusks	huge
gray	eyes
ears	legs

Write information about the elephants.

The elephants are _____. This is how they look; they have _____.

_____
_____
_____
_____
_____
_____
_____

Information Animal Writing Prompts

Word Bank

fish	orange
beak	white
feathers	eyes
gray	long

Write information about the stork.

The stork eats _____. This is how it looks; it has _____.

_____
_____
_____
_____
_____
_____
_____

© A World of Language Learners

Information Animal Writing Prompts

Word Bank	
grazing	head
eating	legs
grass	ears
white	wool

Write information about the sheep.

The sheep are _____. This is how they look; they have _____.

_____
_____
_____
_____
_____
_____
_____
_____

Information Animal Writing Prompts

Word Bank

holding	white
back	tree
fur	arms
tough	legs
eyes	big
nose	mother
gray	joey

Write information about the baby koala.

The baby koala is _____. This is how it looks; it has _____.

_____
_____
_____
_____
_____
_____
_____

Information Animal Writing Prompts

Word Bank

ridding	eyes
pouch	nose
mother	claws
fur	hands
brown	feet
ears	joey

Write information about the baby kangaroo.

The baby kangaroo is _____. This is how it looks; it has _____.

_____
_____
_____
_____
_____
_____
_____
_____

© A World of Language Learners

Point of View Writing Prompts

Point of view is the position that a story is told from.

In first person point of view, the character is telling the story. Use words such as: I, me, my, mine, we.

In third person point of view, the writer is telling about a different character, use words such as: he, she, they, it, ours.

Point of View Writing Prompts

Point of View	
First Person	Third Person
I	he
me	she
my	it
mine	they
we	ours

Word Bank	
blow	splash
pop	wand
funny	wet
wave	eyes
sticky	hand
sky	bubbles

Describe the bubbles.

Write from the point of view of the girl blowing the bubbles.

The bubbles are _____. I feel _____.

_____
_____
_____
_____

Write from the point of view of someone watching..

The bubbles look _____. She is _____.

_____
_____
_____
_____

Point of View Writing Prompts

Point of View		Word Bank	
First Person	Third Person	balance	long
I	he	heavy	fast
me	she	fall	win
my	it	race	grass
mine	they	fun	trip
we	ours	kids	turn
		play	enjoy

Describe the game.

Write from the point of view of the boy with the book on his head.

> I _____ this game. The book feels _____.

_____
_____
_____
_____
_____

Write from the point of view of one of the kids watching.

> The game looks _____. I feel _____.

_____
_____
_____
_____
_____

© A World of Language Learners

Point of View Writing Prompts

Point of View		Word Bank	
First Person	Third Person		
I	he	hit	fall
me	she	catch	injure
my	it	ball	win
mine	they	bat	out
we	ours	run	dirt
		hurt	mitt
		base	helmet

Describe the baseball game.

Write from the point of view of the boy with the child hitting the ball.

I hope that I _____. I feel _____.

_____
_____
_____
_____
_____

Write from the point of view of one of the catcher.

I hope that he/she/they _____. I feel _____.

_____
_____
_____
_____
_____

Point of View Writing Prompts

Point of View		Word Bank	
First Person	Third Person	look	eyes
I	he	special	light
me	she	camera	flash
my	it	distance	kids
mine	they	picture	see
we	ours		

Describe taking a picture.

Write from the point of view of the kid with the camera.

> I hope that I _____. I feel _____.

_____
_____
_____
_____
_____

Write from the point of view of one of the kids standing behind the camera.

> I can see _____. I hope that he/she/they _____.

_____
_____
_____
_____
_____

© A World of Language Learners

Point of View Writing Prompts

Point of View	
First Person	Third Person
I	he
me	she
my	it
mine	they
we	ours

Word Bank	
sand	push
truck	pull
shovel	rough
fill	yellow
heavy	green
hand	brown

Write about filling a truck with sand.

Write from the point of view of the child filling the truck.

I am _____. It _____.

_____
_____
_____
_____
_____

Write from the point of view of the truck.

I am _____. It feels _____.

_____
_____
_____
_____
_____

© A World of Language Learners

Point of View Writing Prompts

Point of View		Word Bank	
First Person	Third Person	long	fun
I	he	horse	full
me	she	heavy	float
my	it	buy	string
mine	they	pretty	holding
we	ours	street	money

Write about the balloons.

Write from the point of view of the person holding the balloons.

I am _____. They are _____.

_____
_____
_____
_____
_____

Write from the point of view of a kid walking past.

I see _____. They are _____.

_____
_____
_____
_____
_____

Point of View Writing Prompts

Point of View	
First Person	Third Person
I	he
me	she
my	it
mine	they
we	ours

Word Bank	
toys	build
Legos	trip
messy	hurt
desk	fun
chair	empty

Write about t the room.

Write from the point of view of the person holding the balloons.

I like _____. It is _____.

_____
_____
_____
_____

Write from the point of view of the truck.

This room is _____. You need to _____.

_____
_____
_____
_____

Point of View Writing Prompts

Point of View		Word Bank	
First Person	Third Person	hot	large
I	he	cool	silly
me	she	standing	funny
my	it	walking	eyes
mine	they	furry	stuffy
we	ours	costume	steps

Write about the bear.

Write from the point of view of the person inside the bear suit.

I am _____. It is _____. I feel _____.

_____
_____
_____
_____
_____

Write from the point of view of the person walking past.

I am _____. It is _____. I feel _____.

_____
_____
_____
_____
_____

© A World of Language Learners

Point of View Writing Prompts

Point of View		Word Bank	
First Person	Third Person	holding	push
I	he	swinging	legs
me	she	waiting	high
my	it	fun	hands
mine	they	boring	breeze
we	ours	turn	sky

Write about the swing.

Write from the point of view of the kid that is in the swing.

I am _____. It is _____. I see _____.

_____
_____
_____
_____
_____

Write from the point of view of a kid waiting for the swing.

I am _____. It is _____. I see _____.

_____
_____
_____
_____
_____

Point of View Writing Prompts

Point of View	
First Person	Third Person
I	he
me	she
my	it
mine	they
we	ours

Word Bank	
water	sit
wet	stand
eyes	playing
hands	silly
fun	orange
splash	brown

Write about the water.

Write from the point of view of the kid getting splashed.

I am _____. I feel _____.

_____
_____
_____
_____
_____

Write from the point of view of one of the kids splashing

I am _____. I feel _____.

_____
_____
_____
_____
_____

© A World of Language Learners

Point of View Writing Prompts

Point of View	
First Person	Third Person
I	he
me	she
my	it
mine	they
we	ours

Word Bank	
big	friend
trunk	stand
ears	smooth
rough	hungry
hug	brown
black	large

Write about the elephant.

Write from the point of view of the child.

I see _____. It is _____. It feels _____.

_____
_____
_____
_____
_____

Write from the point of view of the elephant.

I see _____. It is _____. It feels _____.

_____
_____
_____
_____
_____

© A World of Language Learners

Point of View Writing Prompts

Point of View		Word Bank	
First Person	Third Person		
I	he	ball	hurt
me	she	net	fall
my	it	foot	goal
mine	they	kicking	win
we	ours	catch	lose
		fun	grass

Write about soccer.

Write from the point of view of the goalie.

I see _____. I am _____. I feel _____.

_____
_____
_____
_____
_____

Write from the point of view of the kid kicking the ball.

I see _____. I am _____. I feel _____.

_____
_____
_____
_____
_____

Point of View Writing Prompts

Point of View		Word Bank	
First Person	Third Person	playground	fun
I	he	climb	tower
me	she	hold	bars
my	it	high	hand
mine	they	fall	feet
we	ours	hurt	fall
		smooth	brown

Write about a playground.

Write from the point of view of the child climbing.

I see _____. It is _____. It feels _____.

_____
_____
_____
_____
_____

Write from the point of view of the child standing.

I see _____. It is _____. It feels _____.

_____
_____
_____
_____
_____

© A World of Language Learners

 Point of View Writing Prompts

Point of View	
First Person	Third Person
I	he
me	she
my	it
mine	they
we	ours

Word Bank	
sit	breeze
high	hold
fast	pull
fun	push
boring	chair

Write about the swings.

Write from the point of view of a person riding.

I am _____. I feel _____.

_____
_____
_____
_____
_____

Write from the point of view of the ride operator.

I am _____. I feel _____.

_____
_____
_____
_____
_____

Point of View Writing Prompts

Point of View	
First Person	Third Person
I	he
me	she
my	it
mine	they
we	ours

Word Bank

standing	grass
mountains	hot
saddle	walking
relaxed	hair
bumpy	tired
riding	reins

Write about the horse.

Write from the point of view of the person riding.

I am _____. I feel _____. I see _____.

_____
_____
_____
_____
_____

Write from the point of view of the horse.

I am _____. I feel _____. I see _____.

_____
_____
_____
_____
_____

© A World of Language Learners

Point of View Writing Prompts

Point of View		Word Bank	
First Person	Third Person	point	answer
I	he	raise	call
me	she	hand	excited
my	it	question	teacher
mine	they	desk	correct
we	ours		

Write about the classroom.

Write from the point of view of the student in the front of the room.

I see _____. I feel _____. I want _____.

_____
_____
_____
_____

Write from the point of view of the student at the back of the room.

I see _____. It is _____. It want _____.

_____
_____
_____
_____

© A World of Language Learners

Copyrighted Materials: All Rights Reserved
©A World of Language Learners 2025

Terms of Use

Thank you for purchasing this product.
The contents are the property of Ellie Tiemann and licensed to you only for classroom/personal use as a single user. I retain the copyright, and reserve all rights to this product.

You may not claim this work as your own, giveaway, or sell any portion of this product. You may not share this product anywhere on the internet or on school share sites.

Find a printable pdf version at
https://aworldoflanguagelearners.store/

Find more teaching resources at
https://www.teacherspayteachers.com/Store/A-World-Of-Language-Learners

Get weekly tips and find out about teaching resources at
https://www.aworldoflanguagelearners.com/newsletter/

www.ingramcontent.com/pod-product-compliance
Lightning Source LLC
Chambersburg PA
CBHW050455110426
42743CB00017B/3375